BENEDICT OF NURSIA

Benedict of Nursia

His Message for Today

Anselm Grün, O.S.B.

Translated by Linda M. Maloney

LITURGICAL PRESS
Collegeville, Minnesota

www.litpress.org

Cover design by David Manahan, o.s.b. Illustration: Fresco of S. Bene-detto by Pietro Annigoni at Monte Cassino, Italy.

Originally published as *Benedikt von Nursia: seine Botschaft heute*, no. 7 in the series Münsterschwarzacher Kleinschriften, edited by the monks of the Abbey of Münsterschwarzach. © by Vier-Türme GmbH, Verlag, D-97359 Münsterschwarzach Abtei. All rights reserved. Translated from the seventh revised and updated edition of 2004.

2   3   4   5   6   7   8

Library of Congress Catalog-in Publication Data

Grün, Anselm.
   [Benedikt von Nursia (1979). English]
   Benedict of Nursia : his message for today / Anselm Grün ; trans-lated by Linda M. Maloney.
      p.   cm.
   Includes bibliographical references.
   ISBN-13: 978-0-8146-2910-9 (pbk. : alk. paper)
   ISBN-10: 0-8146-2910-5 (pbk. : alk. paper)
   1. Benedict, Saint, Abbot of Monte Cassino.   2. Benedict, Saint, Abbot of Monte Cassino. Regula.   I. Title.

BR1720.B45G7813   2006
271'.102—dc22

                                                    2005015078

Contents

INTRODUCTION

When guests come to us in the monastery for a few days they are often fascinated by the clear structure of the days, and they sense something of the benevolent spirit of Benedict that shapes our lives. But when they are at home again they do not know how to rescue something of this spirit of Benedict in their daily lives. They are in search of forms for their life that fit, and that let them breathe freely. They suffer from the collapse of the tradition, something they experience in their parishes. Although for the most part they are not conservative, they still miss, in their congregations, the connection to the roots out of which we Christians live. In the monastery they saw that one can live from Benedict's roots without simply clinging to what is old. They sense that tradition is also a blessing. And when our faith neglects its roots it quickly becomes superficial and banal.

Benedict does not have an answer to all the questions that haunt us today. But when we consider Benedict against the background of his chaotic times, his advice acquires a new immediacy for us. The era of globalization resembles Benedict's time, the era of the great tribal migrations, in many respects. Our times are characterized by continuous flexibility, but often the soul is not engaged. It reacts with depression, showing that it lacks security and clarity. Benedict responded to the continual changes of his own time with the demand for *stabilitas*, stability. He accepted people from various tribes and nations into his community, and so contributed to the integration of strangers. He responded to the restless curiosity of his time, the constant search for "events," for *panem et circenses*, bread and games, with a retreat into silence. So I hope that readers will find in Benedict's message an answer to some of their questions and their longings.

I. Benedict Himself

BENEDICT HIMSELF

When we are still talking about someone 1,500 years after his lifetime, when we even refer to him with titles like "Father of Western Civilization" or "Patron of Europe," he must have been a remarkable person. But when we look back into history and try to present a picture of Benedict we are quickly disappointed. The historical data about Benedict's life and work are uncertain and do not yield enough information to allow us a clear picture of this man. The person of Benedict constantly escapes our grasp. We cannot produce as clear a depiction as we can of, for example, St. Francis of Assisi. What stands in the foreground is not the person of Benedict, but his work. Benedict himself disappears behind the work; his life continues in his rule for monasteries, the *Regula Benedicti (RB)*. Through it he continues his effectiveness, and even today he shapes the lives of thousands of male and female monastics throughout the world. Benedict has shaped a model of life that has been accepted over and over again through the centuries with gratitude and is seen as a way for human beings to mature as disciples of Christ.

What kind of person was this, that his advice should continue to be valid throughout 1,500 years and go on forming people even today? It is true that we know few details of Benedict's life that have secure historical attestation. But we know his essence. For through the instructions in his *Rule* shines the essence of the one who could give such instruction. We can see from the words of the *Rule* that Benedict must have been a man of experience, one who knew the weaknesses and strengths of human beings from his own observation, who was at one with himself, balanced, able to lead others, to heal the sick and the weak, to bestow on them courage and hope, a man at peace within himself who knew how to reconcile others and to create around himself an atmosphere of peace. And he must have been a man filled with faith, for in the midst of a world collapsing in on itself he was able to undertake, confidently and without complaining about the terrible times in which he lived, to build up a community of monks.

The life of Benedict can be quickly told. Around the year 480 he was born in Nursia, present-day Norcia, in the Sabine hills of central Italy. As a young man he went to Rome to study, at a time when Rome had lost its significance as the capital of the empire and was in a shabby state. Disgusted at the moral decline of the city, Benedict interrupted his studies and withdrew into solitude. First he joined an ascetic community in Affile, but after a short time he left the community and concealed himself for three years in a cave near Subiaco.

The cave was like a womb in which Benedict experienced rebirth. But like every birth, this one was also painful. First he had to face the truth about himself, his shadow side, his fears, his mortality. He lived through the spiritual steps of experience known to Eastern monasticism. The first Christian monks, who retreated in the fourth century into the desert regions of Egypt, confronted themselves in radical fashion with their own reality. In doing so, they found themselves attacked by demons. These demons were, for them, images of all the passions and emotions that threaten to overwhelm us all. Slowly and painfully they learned how to deal rightly with passions. Benedict, in the cave of Subiaco, experienced peril to his humanity and at the same time underwent a new birth.

"While the saint was alone, the tempter came." Thus Pope Gregory, in the second book of his *Dialogues*, a biography of the father of monastics, summarized this epoch in Benedict's life. In his cave Benedict confronted the storms of passion and fought against them. He emerged the victor, finding his way to peace and harmony with himself. From now on he exuded peace and calm. He emerged from his cave like one newly born.

Benedict's victory over the attacks launched against human existence enabled him to become a teacher for others. Now people found their way to him, first of all shepherds from the neighborhood. They wanted to hear the message of Christ from him. A nearby monastery heard of his reputation and elected him its leader. But apparently Benedict was too strict for these monks. After a while they tried to poison him in order to get rid of him and go on living their bourgeois lives with religious trimming. Benedict left that monastery and went "back to the wilderness he loved, to live alone with himself in the presence of his heavenly Father."[1] "He lived alone," "he returned to himself," "he was alone with himself"—with these words Gregory indicates an essential attitude of the saints. Benedict was alone, that is, with himself; he did not scatter himself around through actions. In his deeds also he remained within himself; he was entirely in his doing without thereby allowing himself to be drawn out of his center. He was in touch with his inner core, his true self. He was in touch with the inner world of his soul. It was from that center that his activity arose.

Benedict's breakthrough to become a person who was entirely self-contained and in harmony with himself was not without effect on his surroundings. Now students began to gather around him, not called by him, but, as Gregory says, brought together by God. For them he founded twelve small monasteries, to each of which he gave an *Abbas*, an experienced monk and "father," as its leader. He himself supervised all of them. The monastic colony bloomed. More and more of the Roman nobility brought their sons to Benedict to be educated. But this aroused the envy of a neighboring priest. He sent young girls to dance in front of the monks' cells to tempt them. Benedict withdrew from the priest's pestering and

---

[1] Gregory the Great, *Life and Miracles of Saint Benedict* (Book 2 of the Dialogues), trans. Odo J. Zimmermann, o.s.b., and Benedict R. Avery, o.s.b. (Collegeville: Liturgical Press, n.d.) 11.

moved to Monte Cassino. Tradition says that Monte Cassino was founded in the year 529, the same year in which the pagan school of philosophy in Athens closed its doors. A new school arose, a "school of the Lord," as the *Rule of Benedict* calls it in its Prologue. On the mountain at Cassino, Benedict built a new monastic community and wrote a rule for it. The *Rule* is the most precious thing Benedict has left us. From it emerges who he was at his deepest depth and how he himself lived. Gregory speaks of the unity of rule and life in his biography of Benedict, the *Dialogues:*

> He wrote a Rule for Monks that is remarkable for its discretion and its clarity of language. Anyone who wishes to know more about his life and character can discover in his Rule exactly what he was like as an abbot, for his life could not have differed from his teaching.[2]

For a long time it was believed that the *Rule* was Benedict's own invention. But newer studies have shown that Benedict relied very much on models for his *Rule*, especially the so-called *Regula Magistri*, the monastic rule of an anonymous "Master." Still, it is precisely in comparison to the model that the originality and the true greatness of Benedict can be seen. In contrast to a pessimistic, suspicious, and often rigorous view of humanity in the model, Benedict shows a trustful attitude toward his monks. Trusting in the good core of human beings was anything but a matter of course in a time when hostile parties vied in committing horrors against each other, in which the moral strength of Roman culture was being extinguished and no new initiative toward a peaceful common life for human beings was on the horizon. In this unreliable age, when people lived in fear and mistrust of one another, Benedict ventured to believe in the goodness in human beings and did not lead his monks with suspicious harshness, but in trust, kindness, and brotherly love.

---

[2] Ibid. 74.

A comparison of the *Rule* with its models allows us to draw a picture of its author something like this: Benedict was a balanced person. All his instructions indicate a wise moderation. Benedict does not want to overburden anyone. He knows human weakness; he knows that monastics are still human beings who have to struggle with normal human problems like rivalry, dissatisfaction, bad moods, idleness, strife, and dislike of one another. Benedict looks these weaknesses in the eye; he does not get annoyed that he, as abbot, has to reckon with human deficiencies, but instead tries to confront them and to heal the people who suffer from them. It emerges from Benedict's words that he was not merely a realist, but also an optimist who did not let himself be driven to resignation or cynicism by human weakness, but was able to live calmly and confidently, with a profound sense of humor and a powerful trust in God's grace, in the midst of human confusion. Benedict did not see himself as a spiritual leader who would accomplish proud deeds with his group of monks, but as a doctor whose task it was to heal weak, sick people and enable them to serve in the school of the Lord.

Anyone so balanced and wise had to have fought hard with himself. The wisdom that speaks from the *Rule* gives us an idea of the experiences Benedict had endured with himself. Benedict did not avoid the attacks and perils of evil; in his struggle for inner purity he had looked into the depths of human nature, so that nothing human was foreign to him. But he had also experienced the power of grace, which is able to heal us. And so he became a wise physician who knew how to deal with human beings, not frightening them away by demands that were too high, but accepting them in their weakness and thus being able to heal them.

Benedict's influence in his own lifetime was small. He built up his community and led it until his death, which can probably be dated to the year 547. It is true that Gregory reports Benedict's preaching to the pagan population and tells of his meeting with King Totila of the Goths, who—deeply impressed

by the saint—was less merciless thereafter. But we would seek
in vain in his biography for an influence like that indicated by
titles such as "Father of Western Civilization" or "Patron of Europe." His entire influence flows from the *Regula Benedicti*, and
through it he lives on. In it we can still sense Benedict's spirit
today—a spirit that still conveys freedom and broadminded-
ness, mildness and mercy, strength and clarity.

Benedict does not preach himself and his personal originality; in his *Rule* he points a way, one that thousands of female
and male monastics have followed through the centuries and
found helpful. The *Rule* has never been understood as purely a
way for religious to live. In the Middle Ages it was, rather,
used as a textbook for the education of the sons of the nobility
and as a "mirror for princes," a handbook for wise rule. Apparently it gives voice to experiences that are fruitful for the
education and leadership of human beings. But we can only
understand the spirit of the *Rule* rightly today if we see it not
as a rulebook or set of laws intended to regulate everything
precisely, but as the concretization of our faith in daily life. It
is not a question of following the *Rule* literally, but of understanding the spirit it breathes, so that in this spirit we can take
charge of our lives today.

The story of Benedict's influence encourages us to ask
what Benedict would like to say to us now, what his message
is for today—not simply for monastics, but for all who are in
search of God. We can only select a few characteristic features
of his message that seem important for our situation at this
moment. Every age has a different focus in its consideration of
Benedict. At some times the value he set on manual labor was
emphasized, at others the creative cultural power of his *Rule*,
at still others his love for liturgy, his sense of order, his wise
moderation. Every age expresses its own needs in its view of
Benedict and its longing to overcome those needs. Thus what
emerges is always a subjective image. That is entirely legiti-
mate. But the image must always be measured against the
figure and the words of Benedict himself, so that Benedict is

not compelled to represent things and ideas that have nothing to do with him. Thus in what follows we will let Benedict speak for himself, against the background of the questions that are vital in this present moment as we search for a more profound spiritual life.

II. Benedict's Message

LIVING IN THE PRESENCE OF GOD

In reading spiritual books we continually find complaints about the absence of God. God has become distant to us; we no longer have a sense of God's presence in our lives. People talk of the "secularization" of the world, so that we can no longer experience God. And two paths are suggested: either total worldly engagement, work in the world—or more concretely, action for the sake of other people, more human solidarity as the real duty of Christians—or it is suggested that we should withdraw into our own interiority: meditation as the way into stillness, silence, a separation from the noise of the world. Often these two ways run counter to each other. Those who are active in the world find no time for meditation, and many who are enthusiastic about meditation find concrete engagement on behalf of a better world too banal. We find one attempt to bring the two poles together in the program of the Youth Councils summoned by Roger Schutz, the prior of Taizé: "Struggle and Contemplation." It is an issue of allowing our action to flow from prayer and meditation, so that in our actions as well we are entirely present to ourselves and entirely present to God, as Gregory says of Benedict.

Benedict was able to show us a path to a successful synthesis of action and contemplation, of work motivated by Christianity and spiritual attentiveness, of mysticism and politics, because he recognized no separation between interiority and engagement, between relationship to God and standing within the world. For Benedict, our whole lives take place in the presence of God. Therefore we are dealing with God everywhere, even in entirely worldly things, even in the banal business of daily life. So he requires of the Cellarer, the administrator and financial officer of the community: "He will regard all utensils and goods of the monastery as sacred vessels of the altar."[1] Dealing with tools, the management of property, handling money—all that, for Benedict, is not something profane; it has to do with God. In his order to the Cellarer, Benedict is alluding to a prophecy of Zechariah, who says that "on that day" every cooking pot in Jerusalem will be sacred to the Lord (Zech 14:20-21). Thus the manager is to regard the monastery's property as God's own, as something that points to fulfillment in the reign of God. In managing the things of this world the monastic encounters the God of the promise that is already beginning and is now present. There is no need to first separate oneself from the world in order to be with God; rather, in the world one is also in God, and when handling things one is also present to the Creator of all things.

Benedict shows in the fourth chapter of his *Rule* what life in the presence of God means: "remind yourself . . . that God's gaze is upon you, wherever you may be." And in the seventh chapter he describes in more detail what it means to be seen and examined by God everywhere. The monastic should be aware that

> . . . he is always seen by God in heaven, that his actions everywhere are in God's sight and are reported by angels at every hour. The Prophet indicates this to us when he shows that our thoughts are always present to God, saying: *God searches hearts and minds* (Ps 7:10).[2]

Living in the presence of God means, then, first that I constantly let God look into the innermost chambers of my heart, that I bare before God all my thoughts and feelings so that God may ask me how much I am attached to myself, how ready I am to surrender myself to God. Living in the presence of God is a continual process of purification. All the feelings and thoughts that rise in me during my daily life, at work or at prayer, are

[1] *RB* 31.10.
[2] *RB* 7.13-14.

held up to God's all-penetrating light so that God may shine through them. In this way life before God leads to a deeper and deeper self-knowledge. In God's light nothing remains hidden from us, no unprocessed experiences, no confused feelings, no desires or needs, no thoughts and moods. Living in the presence of God, we encounter ourselves at every turn. God, in turn, confronts us with our own reality so that we can recognize it and allow it to be purified by God.

However, for Benedict life in the presence of God has another aspect as well. God is present to us as one who speaks to us. The initiative comes from God. That is clear in the Prologue to the *Rule* when Benedict writes:

> Let us open our eyes to the light that comes from God, and our ears to the voice from heaven that every day calls out this charge: *If you hear his voice today, do not harden your hearts* (Ps 94[95]:8). And again: *You that have ears to hear, listen to what the Spirit says to the churches* (Rev 2:7). And what does he say? *Come and listen to me, sons; I will teach you the fear of the Lord* (Ps 33[34]:12). *Run while you have the light* of life, *that the darkness* of death *may not overtake you* (John 12:35).

> Seeking his workman in a multitude of people, the Lord calls out to him and lifts his voice again: *Is there anyone here who yearns for life and desires to see good days?* (Ps 33[34]:13) If you hear this and your answer is "I do," God then directs these words to you: If you desire true and eternal life, *keep your tongue free from vicious talk and your lips from all deceit; turn away from evil and do good; let peace be your quest and aim* (Ps 33[34]:14–15). Once you have done this, my *eyes will be upon* you *and my ears will listen* for your *prayers; and even before you ask me, I will say* to you: *Here I am* (Isa 58:9).[3]

God speaks to us before we have asked him. He speaks to us in the words of Scripture. Benedict places the words of Scripture on God's lips in such a way that they are personally addressed to us. This is no abstract word of God, but a word

---

[3] *RB*, Prologue, 9–18.

in which God speaks to me now, concretely, in my present situation. The distance in time between God's speaking in the Bible and ourselves does not exist for Benedict. The words of Scripture are words spoken to us by the God who is present to us today. It is a question of living with and from God's word. With this word God means to illuminate for us the concrete events and problems of the day and to let us experience the divine presence again and again in the course of our daily lives.

When, for example, we are in a meeting in which the emotions and aggressions of the participants get in the way of a substantial conversation, and we remember the words Benedict cites in the Prologue: "Here I am" (Isa 58:9), God's very self will be present in the midst of this hopelessly derailed conversation. God brings another dimension into the poisoned atmosphere of the meeting, changing the situation by letting us, through the experience of divine presence, believe in a solution, in spite of the stubbornness and narrowmindedness of the participants. God's presence relativizes the present state of things and enables us to see the situation from a higher point of view.

God's presence is not something that is always the same; it is not like an impersonal space that surrounds us. Instead, it is like a trusted person who addresses us in ever new ways. Of course, for Benedict, God is also the Spirit who dwells within us and is ever-present to us. But we do not melt into God. We are not dissolved in God. Instead, God always approaches us as a partner, as someone who challenges us. Depending on the situation and the word with which God addresses us, God always encounters us in a new and often surprising way. When we sit silently, alone in our room, we find God in the words "Here I am" differently than when we recall those words in the midst of a quarrel with another person. But we never experience God as a vague atmosphere of the divine; we encounter God always as a person who confronts and challenges us. God wants to change us through the word; God wants to free us from our wrong attitudes and, in the divine word, to fill us with the divine Spirit.

In the chapter on "Humility" Benedict shows that the internal purification process of the monastic is put in motion by the word of God. He describes the monastic's spiritual path in terms of twelve stages of humility. Each stage of this path is headed by a saying from Scripture. The monastic is to practice each of the attitudes demanded by this stepwise path to God by repeating a passage from the word of God. Thus at the second stage she or he is to keep in mind the words: "I have come . . . not to do my own will, but the will of him who sent me" (John 6:38). At the sixth stage she or he is to say to everything that is assigned:

> I was stupid and ignorant;
>   I was like a brute beast
>   toward you.
> Nevertheless I am
>   Continually with you . . . (Ps 72[73]:22-23).

The word of God does not simply tell me what I am to do; it transforms me, working in me what it says. When Benedict has the monastic say in the face of what is hard and unfavorable: "No, in all these things we are more than conquerors through him who loved us" (Rom 8:37; *RB* 7.39), these words help him or her to cope with the excessive demand, not to be broken or embittered by it, but to overcome it, trusting in the Lord and his presence. For Benedict, spiritual life is essentially life in the presence of God, living out of the word of God. Those who again and again allow themselves to be addressed by the word of God will be transformed more and more into what the word expresses; they will be freed from their narrowness and self-love and filled with God's Spirit. The monastic's asceticism consists in permitting oneself to be transformed by the present God and God's word, and thus to grow more and more deeply into the love of Christ.

The idea of living in the presence of God shapes Benedict's instructions on prayer. Because God is the one who speaks to us, we must first open ourselves to God's word, allow ourselves to be addressed. This happens when God's word is read. Nowadays we are in danger of avoiding this stance of being addressed; we think we must ourselves constantly produce prayers and do not notice how wordy our prayers have become. Or we retreat into silence, fleeing from word into wordlessness, thinking that enjoyment of silence is the same thing as encounter with God.

First comes the word of God that addresses me, touches me, calls me into question, wounds and judges me, but also heals and frees me. Both prayer and silence can only be an answer to God's word and may not precede it. Thus Benedict requires that prayer should be frequent, but short. In it the monastic is to respond to the word of God and express his or her readiness to follow God's demands with deeds. Thus we find in Benedict's *Rule* no teaching on mystical prayer, but very sober instruction to open one's daily life to God again and again in every situation. What is crucial is not our doing, but living before God, in God's presence, listening to God's word that addresses us and shows us the way. In prayer the monastic responds that she or he has heard God's word and is now ready to follow it.

But living in the presence of God does not mean constantly thinking about God. That would split us internally and be too much for us. Rather, it is a matter of opening oneself to a reality, surrendering oneself to the God who surrounds one. Thus practicing the presence of God does not consist of training in concentration, but on the contrary, of relaxing, letting oneself rest in the reality of God, in whom we move and are. Therefore this practice must be carried out not so much in the head as in the body.

Our hearts are to rest in the God who is present; our behavior, our posture, our way of speaking, standing, and walking, our internal collectedness in everything we do should witness to the experience of the God who is present. Benedict does not hesitate to write even about how to speak and to give concrete instructions for posture:

> The eleventh step of humility is that a monk speaks gently and without laughter, seriously and with becoming modesty, briefly and reasonably, but without raising his voice, as it is written: "A wise man is known by his few words."[4]

The experience of the presence of God affects even the voice and the attitude of body:

> The twelfth step of humility is that a monk always manifests humility in his bearing no less than in his heart, so that it is evident at the Work of God, in the oratory, the monastery or the garden, on a journey or in the field, or anywhere else. Whether he sits, walks or stands, his head must be bowed and his eyes cast down.[5]

Living in the presence of God, according to Benedict, shapes all realms of human life: prayer, work, interaction with creation, and relationships to other people. "Fellowship," that great slogan of our time, was for Benedict no contradiction to a devout love of God. The social dimension is always already religious, for in the brother as in the sister we encounter Christ himself. Faith in God is made concrete for Benedict in a belief in the good core of the fellow human being. Therefore faith is expressed in a new way of being with one another. That, for Benedict, is the basis of true humanity. It is not an uplifting ideal, but reality that confronts us again and again in daily situations. Thus Benedict says in the chapter on the monastic counsel that the abbot is to call all the brothers to counsel because "the Lord often reveals what is better to the younger."[6] For Benedict, then, it is clear that the Lord speaks to us through people, that he can speak to us through anyone, even a younger person who may have less experience and knowledge.

Benedict did not write any uplifting thoughts about the encounter with Christ in the brother; he simply takes it for

[4] *RB* 7.60–61.
[5] *RB* 7.62–63.
[6] *RB* 3.3.

granted. It is for him an obvious reality that continually shapes his concrete instructions. Thus he writes:

> Care of the sick must rank above and before all else, so that they may truly be served as Christ, for he said: *I was sick and you visited me* (Matt 25:36), and, *What you did for one of these least brothers you did for me* (Matt 25:40).[7]

The fact that the instructions in the *Rule*, which for long stretches are very down-to-earth, are repeatedly interrupted by such reasoning shows that Benedict lives entirely through faith in the presence of Christ in the brother and sister. It is a faith that is not reserved for unusual situations, but is to be lived in daily life, a faith that marks our ordinary dealings with one another. This is still clearer when Benedict speaks of the reception of guests:

> All guests who present themselves are to be welcomed as Christ, for he himself will say: *I was a stranger and you welcomed me* (Matt 25:35).[8]

Indeed, one ought to bow the head before them or throw oneself on the ground: "Christ is to be adored because he is indeed welcomed in them."[9] When Benedict writes that guests should never be absent from the monastery, that it is thus an ordinary daily affair that guests should come, it is clear how faith in the presence of Christ in the brother and sister shapes the monastic's whole life. It is true that today we can also be inspired by this idea to some edifying actions, but for the most part it stops with edifying ideas. For Benedict, in contrast, the presence of Christ in the brother and sister is reality, just as real as the fact that work in the kitchen, where food is prepared for and served to the guests, is too much for a single brother. Benedict describes the attitude to the guest, in whom

---

[7] *RB* 36.1–3.
[8] *RB* 53.1.
[9] *RB* 53.7.

Christ encounters us, just as soberly as he does the work in the guests' kitchen.

Thus Benedict could help us to be serious about our faith in the presence of Christ in the brother and sister, to approach each other in and out of this faith, and to approach interpersonal problems, tensions, antipathies, and aggressions out of that faith in the reality of Christ in the other. We sense that simply insuperable barriers are built up within us at this point. And with a good deal of reason and logic we then always find adequate reasons for not seeing things so simply, for making distinctions, and so on. Benedict speaks out of his faith in the presence of God as if it were the most natural thing in the world. And perhaps that can help us to dare, beyond our clear reasoning, beyond our excuses, to take a step toward reality and to take the presence of Christ in our brother and sister so seriously that it will shape our attitudes, our behavior, our words, and our views.

ORA ET LABORA—
PRAYER AND WORK

The link between prayer and work—the management of work in light of prayer—as described by Benedict in his *Rule* is an important message especially for people today, because many people feel themselves simply overburdened by work. Everywhere you go, you hear complaints about the stress imposed by work. Work appears to alienate people, to irritate them. In a countercurrent against overwork, it seems that many people are trying to leave the work world. In their search for an alternative lifestyle they are not trying just to live more simply, but frequently also to work less, sometimes so little that they cannot even earn enough to support their simpler lifestyle. It is especially groups that are seeking a deeper religious experience that frequently believe they can only do so by reducing their workload.

Benedict sees no contradiction between work and prayer. He has the monastics work about five hours a day in winter and eight hours in summer, enough so that they can earn their own living. But more crucial than a balanced partnership of prayer and work is their internal connection. Work is to help us to pray well, and prayer is to help us to do our work well. And in the end work, rightly understood, should itself become prayer.

Work helps us to pray. In the chapter on manual labor Benedict writes: "Idleness is the enemy of the soul. Therefore, the brothers should have specified periods for manual labor as well as for prayerful reading."[1] Work, then, defends against idleness. That does not appear to be much help to praying, and

[1] *RB* 48.1.

yet behind it lies the following experience: In their attempt to live in the presence of God, monastics continually find that they attempt to flee from that reality by withdrawing, through imagination, into an illusory world. In the world of fantasy it is not God, but one's own ego that is in the foreground. And so Pope Gregory sees it as a sign of pride when someone "goes walking alone with himself in the broad places of his imagination."[2] Insofar as work demands my whole attention and ties my thoughts to what I am doing right now it keeps me from fleeing into the illusory world of imagination and helps me to maintain my status as one bound to God. The collected state into which a concentrated effort, done without haste, brings me thus also deepens my collectedness in prayer.

For Benedict prayer has the first place, and only out of prayer can I manage my work in such a way that it has a positive effect on my religious life. Prayer relieves us from the load of work. Many people never stop working because they see it as too important. They ponder over and over whether they have done everything correctly, whether they have forgotten anything, what others would say, whether they will get a good evaluation, and so on. These musings cramp us internally and put crushing demands on us. In prayer we let go of work. We have tried our best while working, but now we leave it to God to make something of it. Prayer frees us from too much concern about our work. It makes us free to live entirely in the present, to be wholly present to our work but then to put aside our work so that it no longer occupies us internally.

Prayer also clarifies the motives that impel us to work. Many problems with our work arise from the fact that we have not clarified our motives. Feelings of displeasure, feelings of being exploited and overloaded, often have their roots in unclarified motives. When we bare these feelings before God in prayer we will discover what is wrong with us, where we are refusing to accept something God is offering us. We will

---

[2] J. P. Migne, ed., *Patrologia Latina* (MPL) (Turnhout: Brepols, 1967) 76:745a.

sometimes realize that we do not want to let ourselves be challenged by God; instead, we compare ourselves to others and feel disadvantaged instead of surrendering ourselves to what God has planned for us.

Benedict puts great value on working for pure motives. For him, motivation for work is more important than success. He writes:

> If there are artisans in the monastery, they are to practice their craft with all humility, but only with the abbot's permission. If one of them becomes puffed up by his skillfulness in his craft, and feels that he is conferring something on the monastery, he is to be removed from practicing his craft and not allowed to resume it unless, after manifesting his humility, he is so ordered by the abbot.[3]

Work is only worship if I am not attached to it, if I do not misuse it for my own self-satisfaction or to obtain public approval. Benedict seeks the same attitude in work as in prayer, that is, humility and readiness to surrender to God's will and to serve not oneself, but God. Whether someone is serving God by his or her work, or only the self, is concretely evident from whether the person is prepared to undertake a different work when the needs of the community require it. Work, as Benedict understands it, demands self-renunciation, and only when it is done out of selfless love does it glorify God, just as prayer does.

Most of our difficulties at work come from our coworkers. One is too slow and has a hard time understanding, another gets on our nerves by talking constantly. Here prayer can help us to arrive at a more positive attitude toward our coworkers. When we pray for them, give thanks for them, we will spread a more humane work atmosphere around us and we ourselves will get along better with our fellow human beings.

Ultimately, Benedict sees prayer and work as a unity, and this especially because of his idea of the presence of God. Work

[3] *RB* 57.1–3.

itself becomes prayer when it is done in the presence of God. When I work in the presence of God, I respond to God with my actions. Then I can give myself entirely to work without being divided in my head, for devoting myself to work is done in obedience to God and as a response to God's presence. Here, too, the presence of God shapes the way I work. Those who work hastily and carelessly, trying to finish everything as quickly as possible, are constantly slipping out of the presence of God. Working in the presence of God requires that I work with inner peace and without haste, out of my own center, collected, giving myself entirely to the work. The attentiveness that many spiritual writers refer to nowadays is, for Benedict, the basic attitude required by every action.

In the directions to the Cellarer quoted above, to treat the utensils and property of the monastery like the sacred altar vessels, Benedict shows that the monastic is constantly dealing with God in whatever she or he does. This statement expresses the reverence Benedict felt toward all things. Because we come across traces of God everywhere in the world, we can treat the world with reverence. We have become alert to this message today in light of the destruction of our environment. In Benedict's time, too, there was thoughtless exploitation of the human environment. Fields were stripped by wandering sheep, forests were felled for military purposes. The land lay fallow. People's hatred for one another had also destroyed Nature. In the midst of an economy that had fallen into chaos Benedict created, with his monastery, some tiny, self-sufficient economic units that extended from primary agricultural production through manual processing to the most varied types of services. These economic units were not governed by the principle of maximizing profit; instead, glorifying God was the highest principle. Benedict requires of his monastics that they sell their products more cheaply than the people of the world, "that God may be glorified in all things . . . ."[4] It is not maximizing

[4] 1 Peter 4:11; *RB* 57.9.

profit and exploiting the world, but reverence for things and praise of the Creator of all things that are to shape the work of monastics. Work must not destroy the world; instead, it must treat it in such a way that it reflects and praises its Creator. In our work we are to make the world transparent to the Creator. That only happens when we listen to God's word in things, to God's purpose for the world, and when we regard the world not as our property, but as something entrusted to us by God. The things of the world proclaim their Creator, and they point to the end-time when everything will be holy and belong to the Lord.

It seems to me that Benedict's joining of prayer and work is crucially important especially for people today. We cannot simply withdraw from the work world. But work is also more than a necessary evil without which we could not earn our living. When we join prayer and work, then work will also be for us a place of spiritual life, a place that does not separate us from God but in which we can practice the right attitude toward God: obedience, patience, confidence, trust, selflessness, and love. For many, a flight from work is also a flight from the realities of life and therefore a flight from God. Benedict could teach us to manage our work on the basis of prayer and to see work itself as prayer, in which, as we work, we place ourselves before the God who is present to us and permit ourselves to be supported by God even in the tiredness of our bodies.

When we work out of prayer we will still get tired, but we will not be exhausted. It is a good tiredness. We have the feeling of having done something for God and other people. Exhaustion, on the other hand, creates emptiness, dissatisfaction, restlessness. In prayer we come into contact with the inner source of the Holy Spirit, which is inexhaustible because it comes forth from God.

DISCRETIO—
THE GIFT OF DISCERNMENT

Another of Benedict's characteristics is his high esteem for *discretio*, for the correct assessment, the gift of discernment of spirits. Today the religious situation is marked by the two poles of laxity and rigorism. The many sectarian youth groups, gruesome reports of mass murders of fanatic adherents of sects—these are as alarming as the rapid breakdown of traditions in families and congregations. On the one extreme, many are enthused by rigorous demands and manifestations of religious living. In contrast, Benedict's *discretio* can be dismissed as mediocrity. It is true that Benedict's message is hardly likely to evoke waves of enthusiasm. It refrains from exalted ideals in order, through wise moderation, to meet the needs of human beings. The preaching of high ideals always runs the risk of offering people a way of identification that is, at the same time, an invitation to flee from oneself, since it suggests flight from one's own negative side. Young people especially, who already suffer from feelings of inferiority, expect by identifying with a high ideal to achieve an increased sense of self-worth. In the short run it can even be helpful to identify with a high ideal. It can give stability to those who are fragile. But in the long run it will not lead to maturity; instead, it will narrow their lives in such a way that they are kept in a state of immaturity or are shattered. In their brokenness, many then throw all ideals overboard and refuse to be inspired by anything again.

Benedict did not need to use psychological tricks to bring people into his community. He describes his hopes for monastic life in very sober terms:

> Therefore we intend to establish a school for the Lord's service. In drawing up its regulations, we hope to set down nothing

harsh, nothing burdensome. The good of all concerned, however, may prompt us to a little strictness in order to amend faults and to safeguard love. Do not be daunted immediately by fear and run away from the road that leads to salvation. It is bound to be narrow at the outset.[1]

What is to be sought after is neither an ideal nor an achievement; all the instructions are for the sake of human beings and their salvation. For Benedict, the focus is on human beings. They are to be made whole and find the path to life. The human being is not functionalized or subjected to the dictates of achievement, not even religious achievement. Benedict does not call his members to the service of God or other people by trumpeting the great works the monastery will achieve. For Benedict, such an advertisement would be an orientation to the external, a self-subjection to the standards of achievement. Benedict wants to be fair to human beings, including and especially the weaker ones. He accepts people as they are, including the weak. He does not preach a religion of the strong. He avoids the enthusiasm that can be evoked by exaggeration of demands. He reckons with human weaknesses and wants to lead the weak, also, to life. That requires a path of wise moderation, measured not on self-concocted ideals, but on concrete men and women. But for this very reason Benedict's instruction is an offer of life for very many. Benedict does not frighten; he gives courage, he offers a hand up. Despite his realism—for he knows all human weaknesses from his own experience—he remains an optimist who promises especially to the weak, the difficult types, the average, those who are irritated by banal conflicts, that they will find the path of life.

However, *discretio* is by no means a simple adaptation to the current lifestyle, to the standards and maxims of our society. It would be a fatal misunderstanding of Benedict's intentions to misuse *discretio* to justify a middle-class lifestyle in

---

[1] *RB*, Prologue, 45–48.

the monastery. At any rate, a bourgeois monasticism cannot appeal to Benedict for justification. Rather, Benedict sees *discretio* as the virtue of arranging all things in such a way that the strong are attracted and the weak are not frightened away (cf. *RB* 64.19). The strong are not simply to adapt to the level of the weak; instead, they are to be supported in their efforts, but in such a way that the weak are not discouraged thereby, but rather are encouraged. The strong must carry the weak along with them. For the ancient monastics that is the sign of real strength. And psychology tells us the same thing today: Only those who are strong enough to accept their own weaknesses can bear with and support the weak. We get so annoyed about the weak because, in the best case, they remind us of our own weaknesses, so painfully overcome, that we would prefer to have nothing more to do with. Benedict challenges the strong in his community to bear with the weak without setting themselves above them, but instead out of their knowledge of their own weakness and in gratitude for God's help, which is always received only so that we can hand it on to others. Thus Benedict is not interested in reducing the challenges, but in encouragement and motivation for both weak and strong. This prevents a splitting of the community into "solid achievers" and "lesser achievers," and binds all within the grace of God, which they know is their true support.

Discretio, as the gift of discernment, is especially a virtue of the abbot, the virtue of each of those who are to lead and guide, instruct and educate others. Thus Benedict demands of the abbot:

> . . . he must show forethought and consideration in his orders, and whether the task he assigns concerns God or the world, he should be discerning and moderate, bearing in mind the discretion of holy Jacob, who said: *If I drive my flocks too hard, they will all die in a single day* (Gen 33:13).[2]

[2] *RB* 64.17–18.

The gift of discernment does not simply assume a good assessment of the situation or much in the way of knowledge and
experience, but above all a distance from oneself. The judgment
should not be clouded by one's own ego, one's own desires
and needs. It must be free of what psychology nowadays calls
"projection": of unresolved problems, emotions, and drives
that one does not clearly discern within oneself and therefore
projects into the world outside. *Discretio* therefore presupposes
that one has come, through careful self-observation, to know
oneself and one's own needs, and has seen through one's own
emotions and aggressions.

For the ancient monastics, *discretio* was the discernment of
spirits. This is a gift that, while it presupposes a consistent
self-observation, is ultimately the gift of God's grace. One
must question one's own thoughts regarding the spirit that
shows itself therein: Do I allow myself to be led by my own
spirit, or by the Spirit of God? Where do these various desires
and internal drives come from? Are they from God or from
the Evil One? Ultimately one can achieve the gift of discernment only in a prayerful interaction with God, by penetrating
into the Spirit of God.

The monastics regarded *discretio* as the "mother of all
virtues," and Benedict shared that opinion (cf. *RB* 64.19).
What is new with him is that he applies it not only to spiritual things such as the spiritual direction of a person, where it
is indispensable, but also to daily matters. Worldly business,
for Benedict, also has something to do with God. And one
must clearly distinguish whether in purely material decisions,
too, I am letting myself be led by the Spirit of God or by my
own spirit. Whether I am following God's Spirit or not is
something I can show, for example, in a choice for or against
investing in a machine. As I am to take control of work
through prayer, so I should also make material decisions in
daily life by asking where the Spirit of God is. The divine Spirit
will prevent me from letting my own emotions and unac-
knowledged needs influence my decisions. God's Spirit enables

objectivity. It makes it possible for me to listen to God's voice in things. *Discretio* is thus not an arbitrariness that justifies itself as uncontrollable, because inspired by the Spirit of God, but is a listening to the Spirit of God that speaks to me through things, people, and circumstances, uncovers my own unconscious wishes and needs, and frees me to see God's will in the concrete situation.

Today many people are beginning to listen to the Spirit of God. In the charismatic movement this listening to the Spirit is very important. People only make decisions after they have listened to God in prayer. That is certainly a good thing. However, one gets the impression that sometimes a person's own impulsiveness is confused with the Spirit of God. Some people, appealing to the Spirit, let the ground slip out from under their feet. Benedict can show us, in this situation, how sober one must be in order to possess *discretio*, the mother of virtues, and how soberly one must simultaneously listen to the Spirit of God and the concrete things of daily life, to people and situations. He shows us that human initiatives and listening to the Spirit go together, that it is precisely in the discernment of spirits that I am also enabled to judge and decide more practically and more appropriately for the human condition. For Benedict, the discernment of spirits has nothing rapturous about it. One needs only to read his commands to the abbot in order to sense that here, at all times, one needs to have one's feet on the ground, and that nevertheless the Spirit of God shines through the whole. A couple of passages should make this clear:

> He must hate faults but love the brothers. When he must punish them, he should use prudence and avoid extremes; otherwise, by rubbing too hard to remove the rust, he may break the vessel. He is to distrust his own frailty and remember *not to crush the bruised reed* (Isa 42:3). By this we do not mean that he should allow faults to flourish, but rather, as we have already said, he should prune them away with prudence and love as he sees best for each individual. Let him strive to be loved rather

than feared. Excitable, anxious, extreme, obstinate, jealous or oversuspicious he must not be. Such a man is never at rest.[3]

The abbot must always remember what he is and remember what he is called, aware that more will be expected of a man to whom more has been entrusted. He must know what a difficult and demanding burden he has undertaken: directing souls and serving a variety of temperaments, coaxing, reproving and encouraging them as appropriate. He must so accommodate and adapt himself to each one's character and intelligence that he will not only keep the flock entrusted to his care from dwindling, but will rejoice in the increase of a good flock.[4]

It is clear from these statements that Benedict is not oriented to abstract ideals or rigid principles. His concern is with human beings. The abbot or abbess must be fair to individuals, taking the individual where he or she finds them and constantly inquiring about the will of God in each concrete situation. *Discretio* brings order and clarity into common life, but it does without strict rules and principles. It is easier for anyone who has to do with human beings to stick to fixed principles than to deal with each person individually. But continually appealing to our principles and hiding behind them is a sign of our own fear and insecurity. Because we are anxious about our own fragility, we hide behind principles without noticing that we are subjecting ourselves and our surroundings to those principles and are thereby enslaving ourselves.

Benedict's *discretio* has no interest in strict standards. Benedict approaches each individual and accommodates himself to the uniqueness of each. It is true that he establishes basic principles, but he continually breaks them in order to take account of concrete people and particular situations. He subjects everything to the wise judgment of the abbot or abbess and not to a rule established once and for all. This expresses an enormous trust in the ability of people to judge, an

[3] *RB* 64.11–16.
[4] *RB* 2.30–32.

ability that draws from the discernment of spirits and listening to the Spirit of God in order to be able to discern clearly and make decisions. Behind these statements stands the experience of one's own fragility and at the same time the experience of divine grace, which bears with us in our weaknesses and enables us to bear with one another.

It is no accident that for centuries Benedict's *Rule* was *the* textbook for the education of the young. *Discretio* as the maxim of all education could also do more justice to young people today than many pedagogical theories oriented to abstract ideals and not to concrete people. Sometimes one gets the impression that students are being pressed into the mold of pedagogical concepts instead of having their real needs heard. Many of the things the various Departments of Education propound as pedagogical guidelines sound good, but often these concepts did not arise from listening to young people. They were, rather, produced out of scholarly reasoning that sounds entirely plausible, but too often has no application to concrete human beings. In accompanying young people through courses and retreats I myself have discovered how, by listening to these young men and women, I have received a different message than I got from reading sociological books about teenagers and young adults.

But above all, Benedictine *discretio* could help us to be more humane with one another. Nowadays we are running the risk of judging other people according to psychological criteria and then always wanting to change them if they do not correspond to the criteria. We no longer notice how we subject each other to external standards, how we think we know exactly what is normal and what is good for other people. We can learn from Benedict to let go of all our psychological theories, which too often muddy our vision of concrete human beings, in order to encounter individuals openly and impartially and to welcome the unique character of each.

PAX BENEDICTINA—
BENEDICTINE PEACE

T he Benedictine ideal of the human being is not that of
one who achieves and accomplishes things, not a person
with an unusual religious gift, not a great ascetic, but
the wise and mature person who knows how to bring people
together, who creates around herself or himself an atmosphere
of peace and mutual understanding. Behind this ideal image
stands a high demand. No one can simply resolve to become a
peacemaker. Only those who have created peace within themselves can make peace, only those who have become reconciled
with themselves, their own weaknesses and faults, their needs
and desires, their contradictory tendencies and ambitions.
Making peace is not a program of action that one could write
on one's banners; rather, it must arise from inner peace. And
inner peace is achieved only through a hard and unremitting
struggle for inner purity and through prayer, in which one
seeks to accept everything God presents, whether one's own
weaknesses or those of others.

Benedict demands especially of the abbot or abbess that he
or she should be able to make peace. The most important precondition for this is the ability to heal. The abbot or abbess
must prove, above all, to be a good physician in dealing with
weak and sick brothers and sisters. Thus Benedict writes:

> The abbot must exercise the utmost care and concern for way-
> ward brothers, because *it is not the healthy who need a physician,
> but the sick* (Matt 9:12). Therefore, he ought to use every skill
> of a wise physician and send in *senpectae*, that is, mature and
> wise brothers who, under the cloak of secrecy, may support
> the wavering brother, urge him to be humble as a way of mak-

ing satisfaction, and *console him lest he be overwhelmed by exces-sive sorrow* (2 Cor 2:7). Rather, as the Apostle also says: *Let love for him be reaffirmed* (2 Cor 2:8), and let all pray for him.

It is the abbot's responsibility to have great concern and to act with all speed, discernment and diligence in order not to lose any of the sheep entrusted to him. He should realize that he has undertaken care of the sick, not tyranny over the healthy. Let him also fear the threat of the Prophet in which God says: *What you saw to be fat you claimed for yourselves, and what was weak you cast aside* (Ezek 34:3-4). He is to imitate the loving ex-ample of the Good Shepherd who left the ninety-nine sheep in the mountains and went in search of the one sheep that had strayed. So great was his compassion for its weakness that *he mercifully placed it on his sacred shoulders* and so carried it back to the flock (Luke 15:5).[1]

Our normal reaction to the weak who are placed under us is annoyance and anger. We feel that our self-respect is wounded by weak and sick colleagues. Each of us wants to be proud of the community we lead, the abbot of his monastery, the boss of her business firm, the father or mother of his or her family. When there are black sheep in the community, they are pushed to the margins; we prefer not to notice them. Above all, outsiders should not see them, because that would damage the community's reputation. Sometimes we feel our-selves almost personally attacked and insulted if one of our fellow community members misbehaves.

Benedict requires that the abbot or abbess surrender all am-bition regarding the reputation of his or her community and follow the individual in his or her weakness, going after him or her like the good shepherd. In following the other in his or her weakness, the abbot or abbess enters into his or her own weakness and confronts it. And thus one proves to be a true physician, one who permits himself or herself to be wounded by the wounds of the other in other to keep them in God's

---

[1] *RB* 27.

healing love. Therefore the most effective means of the abbatial healing arts is prayer. When all human methods are of no further avail, neither loving attention nor strictness and admonition, then "let him apply an even better remedy: he and all the brothers should pray for him so that the Lord, who can do all things, may bring about the health of the sick brother."[2]

The ability to heal is the precondition for the abbot or abbess to be able to make peace in the community. Peace cannot be dictated or established through discipline; it must grow out of a love that is strong enough to take up and heal all the brothers' and sisters' failings. This demands of the abbot or abbess an extraordinary amount of love. This is the experience of everyone who is the head of a community and must constantly experience the daily frictions and conflicts within it. We are tempted either to suppress the conflicts or habitually to impose a harshness that does not allow them to emerge. Or we resign ourselves and take refuge in irony. We build up a wall within us that separates us from the weak brothers or sisters and leaves us alone in our apparently intact world.

The peace that the abbot or abbess is to create in the community is nothing weak, not a peace that can only be achieved by giving in, but a peace that does not turn away even from the knife of expulsion. The abbot or abbess is not to suppress conflicts, but address them openly. Thus Benedict writes a whole chapter about the admonition and punishment of fallen brothers. And the measures he there recommends seem to us quite drastic. Benedict addresses conflicts with consistency, but not with rigor. His highest maxim is always responsibility even for the weak and the desire to heal them.

For Benedict, peace comes about in a community when each admits his or her own desires and needs, and the abbot or abbess, with the gift of discernment, decides to what degree the needs of individuals can be taken into account.

[2] RB 28.4–5.

> It is written: *Distribution was made to each one as he had need*
> (Acts 4:35). By this we do not imply that there should be fa-
> voritism—God forbid—but rather consideration for weak-
> nesses. Whoever needs less should thank God and not be
> distressed, but whoever needs more should feel humble because
> of his weakness, not self-important because of the kindness
> shown him. In this way all the members will be at peace.[3]

These few sentences contain a whole program for making
peace. The precondition for peace in a community is that each
member is able to deal straightforwardly with his or her own
needs. These needs must not be suppressed, but they must not
be justified by any means available either, and certainly not pre-
sented as demands. A need is always the recognition of a weakness. Nevertheless, needs have their rightful place. Benedict
acknowledges that this should be recognized, but always with
the knowledge that "I need this because I am too weak to do
without it." Because I have not yet reached that point in my
self-control, I need good food for my spiritual balance. Because I do not love God enough, I need warm human com-
panionship for my psychological health. When I thus admit
my needs and accept them in light of my weaknesses I am at
peace with myself, and my needs will not become an attack on
those who do not have them. In turn, those who have fewer
needs, who, for example, can get by with less food, will not be
proud and hold themselves above others. That would only
lead to fruitless comparisons, which ultimately are the cause
of all strife. They are to thank God that they need less, but
without setting themselves above others in doing so. Then the
doing without will create inner joy. Fulfilling needs thankfully
and thankfully being able to do without: here lies the path to
peace with oneself and thus also to peace within a community. And this attitude prevents grumbling, which cripples all
spiritual progress. Because grumbling threatens peace in the
community, Benedict attacks this vice very sharply.

[3] *RB* 34.1–5.

> First and foremost, there must be no word or sign of the evil of grumbling, no manifestation of it for any reason at all. If, however, anyone is caught grumbling, let him undergo more severe discipline.[4]

Grumbling shows that I am dissatisfied with myself. But instead of admitting one's own dissatisfaction, one projects the cause into the community and thus creates conflict and confusion. One feels compelled to criticize everything and everyone, seeking the reasons for unsatisfying conditions in other people—the abbot, the other brothers or sisters who are not keeping the *Rule*. One does not dare to admit that behind this love of criticism lies an unrecognized dissatisfaction with oneself. And yet the constant desire to improve everything often arises out of an unconscious rejection of oneself. Because I cannot bear myself and my weaknesses, I refuse to bear with the weaknesses of others. But real improvement is only possible when it happens out of love, that is, out of the acceptance of one's own weaknesses as well as those of others.

In our time sociologists are documenting an increasing inability to achieve peace. The polarization of groups within society has increased. Parties have become accustomed to using a rougher tone in their dealings with each other. Groups have forgotten how to be objective toward others, to understand and take seriously the just desires of others. People very quickly set up a picture of the other as enemy and fight against it. Those who study the cause of peace are searching for ways in which we can live together in peace in this world of increasing globalization. The future of our world depends on it. In this situation we can learn from Benedict how to practice the ability to be peaceful.

Benedict does not lay out a magnificent program for peace; what he does is to create peace around himself. That is what it is all about for us, too. Every "program" has something com-

---

[4] RB 34.6–7.

bative about it. Today, even in the name of what is good, in the name of positive ideals, programs are set up that are aimed first of all against something or someone. People fight for the Christian family, and in doing so they fight against everyone who has expressed an opinion contrary to their own ideal. There seems to be a need for an enormous expenditure on polemic in order to advocate for something positive. Benedict is a complete stranger to this kind of fight. He does not set himself up against something or someone, but for something—and yet not for abstract ideals or programs, but for concrete people, for his little community at Monte Cassino. In the midst of a world fallen into chaos he builds his community, attempting to make space for the peace of Christ within it. He makes no claim that he is modeling peace for the world. Without any claim to having been sent, he makes Christian life a reality around himself, working day after day to build up a Christian community of life. Walter Nigg calls Benedict "the building person," who, undaunted and indefatigable, simply does the next thing, a person with a completely positive attitude to whom every negative tendency and every kind of polemic is foreign.

To become positive people who can build up without destroying others: this is one of the most important challenges Benedict sets before us today. We should not attempt to establish great programs, because programs can be used to avoid what is concrete and what is right in front of us. It is a matter, instead, of simply doing what we have recognized as good and worthwhile, without always having to aim our actions against someone. Especially in our de-Christianized world we effect very little if we are constantly complaining about de-Christianization. It is a question of living our Christianity without claiming to be the only good people in the world. With Benedict we never hear a word of complaint about the conditions in the church and in the world that seemed so hopeless in his time. Benedict does not sully his strength with accusations, but simply devotes himself to his work. In his little community of monks he tries to make peace a reality. That peace did not seize the entire West all at once. The community at Monte Cassino was much too insignificant for that. But in his attempt to make peace Benedict handed on experiences that had their effect over centuries and made an essential contribution to peace in the Western world of the Middle Ages.

STABILITAS AND ORDER

Historians emphasize that *stabilitas*, stability, binding oneself to a concrete community, which Benedict requires of his monastics, was a medicine for the restless era of the great tribal migrations. In recent years there have been attempts to weaken this *stabilitas*. In this era of mobility it is said to be a relic from the past. But nowadays we are beginning to have a new appreciation for the positive meaning of *stabilitas*. Especially in our restless time, when people are forced to change their residence again and again and to establish themselves in new environments, fixed points are a blessing. A monastery that has been in the same place for centuries is a guarantee of fruitful continuity. A monastery has deep roots in history and so can offer support and security in our rootless times. From this continuity there arises also a certain calmness in the face of the events of these days.

A community of people who remain together for life can be a place of security for many. One can count on finding the same monastics there, going through the same order of things every day. One knows that at this hour the monks or sisters are singing Vespers. Just knowing of the constancy of the life of a monastic community lets us participate in their life. We feel ourselves incorporated into a community and its continuity.

Many young people have developed a sense of the importance of being able to rely on a solid community, of how a community that lives together permanently can offer stability and security. It is more than a couple of agreeable monastics one knows within the community; it is a life supported by generations, handed on from the old to the young, a community carried forward day after ordinary day, through all the years in which, for individuals, so much has changed.

In our days we can observe an increasing aversion to commitment. People are afraid to tie themselves down in marriage; they want to try it out first. People hesitate to choose a profession; they want to leave all their options open. And before they notice it, the doors have closed. So they go on living indecisively and without solid ties. Instead of the more intense and free life they had hoped for, they reap rootlessness, insecurity, fear of living. There are certainly a great many causes for this fear of commitment. One is the lifestyle that is increasingly demanded of people today: flexibility on the job, continually moving from place to place in order to advance in one's profession. Psychologists have observed that depression, appearing more and more frequently nowadays, is the soul's protest against this flexibility. The soul yet senses that it needs solid roots, that it needs stability in order to grow. People are often in the same state as the African bearers who were driven faster and faster by a German safari guide. They stopped and refused to go on because their souls had not caught up with them yet. Today we cannot stand still externally, so nothing remains to us but the soul's protest, expressed as depression.

It may be that an encounter with St. Benedict's *stabilitas* can be a medicine for people who no longer feel at home in these restless times. But Benedictine stability must not be merely flight from confrontation with the challenges of society. It is, rather, a counterweight that invites us to pay attention to our roots, and its purpose is to encourage us to decide, to commit ourselves, to accept ties. It is not much use to say theoretically that every person needs a commitment, because in order to commit myself I must sense sufficient strength and trust in myself. However, it may be that a community of people who have committed themselves, linked themselves so closely together that they can bear each other's weaknesses for a lifetime, can encourage young people to make decisions. Only the experience that blessing can grow out of commitment and decision for others can give someone the confidence necessary to take his or her own step.

But *stabilitas* is more than simply binding oneself and remaining in a single place. For the ancient monastics *stabilitas* was essentially holding fast when all sorts of thoughts and temptations beset one. The counsel of the Desert Fathers and Mothers was always to remain in one's cell and especially not to leave it when one sensed an inner restlessness and depression within oneself. Remaining in the cell means not avoiding one's own problems but facing them, not running away from oneself or fleeing into activities when a confrontation with oneself is seriously required. *Stabilitas* as standing fast, sticking to one's cell, would be a medicine for the inner restlessness of many people today as well.

Pascal once said that "all the unhappiness of men arises from one single fact, that they cannot stay quietly in their own chamber."[1] If we were to learn again how to stay in our room, to endure and to resist the temptation to constant movement, we could sense how many things within us are made more clear, how we can get at the roots of our problems, and how we can discover where our healing can begin. As at the time of the great population migrations, which the Romans hoped to hold in balance through a call for dramatic performances, today also Benedictine *stabilitas* could exercise a healing effect on the restlessness of human beings. We cannot expect to achieve an internal balance from external things or from constant movement, but only from coming to ourselves, dwelling with ourselves, as Gregory so accurately described the life of Benedict.

A further element of Benedictine life is order, the order of the days, which brings a clear structure into the course of daily life, which divides the passing hours between prayer and work, silence and speech, commonality and solitude. Benedict

---

[1] Blaise Pascal, *Thoughts on Religion.* Trans. W. F. Trotter (New York: Collier, 1909) no. 139.

often speaks of the *hora competens*, the proper, the appropriate hour, the right time. And he tells the abbot or abbess to take care that everything is done at the right time:

> It is the abbot's care to announce, day and night, the hour for the Work of God. He may do so personally or delegate the responsibility to a conscientious brother, so that everything may be done at the proper time.[2]

There is a time for everything. The right time for prayer is just as important as the right time for work and the appropriate time at which the brothers or sisters may ask something of the Cellarer:

> Necessary items are to be requested and given at the proper times (lat. *horis competentibus*), so that no one may be disquieted or distressed in the house of God.[3]

Here Benedict says quite clearly why he divides the day so definitively and has everything happen at the appropriate time. The ordering of the day is for the peace of the community and of individuals. No one is to be sad or confused. When there is too hectic a pace and too much uproar, when one cannot rely on anything, apathy takes over within us. We have no more motivation to give ourselves over to work or to community. This, in turn, leads to deepening depression. Benedict does not desire an order that is artificially imposed on people, but an opportunity for individuals to create and find order within themselves. Those who subject themselves to external order learn that thereby they bring order into their own moods and feelings as well, that they put up a barrier to the fickleness of their own hearts that does not simply push something down, but opens up a space in which the heart can become whole.

Order, for Benedict, is a factor in healing. If the community sets itself in good order it is a sign that it is healthy, or that it can become healthy through a healthy ordering. As a rule

[2] *RB* 47.1.
[3] *RB* 31.18–19.

Benedict orders the life of the monastics so precisely because, through a wise external ordering, he wants to establish a kind of defense so that the monastics who subject themselves to this order will be internally ruled by it and will find wholeness. A clear order makes possible a clear life. Many young people are beginning to understand this nowadays. In their search for an alternative lifestyle they provide orders for themselves so as to distinguish their lives, even in purely external things, from those of others. Their lifestyle becomes for them a symbol that they themselves are different. They seek security in the order they set for themselves. In the long run no one can manage without this inner ordering, without the security of a sheltering order; otherwise they will expend energy to no avail. Those who have to find a new system or schedule for living day after day, over and over again, spend their strength unnecessarily. A sensible ordering given once and for all makes us free for the essentials, and it gives us the necessary security to feel at home, not to furnish one's life comfortably, but in order to be able to pursue, with steadiness, the inner process of maturing.

Beyond military drill and a purely external order governed by stiff principles whose sense can no longer be made out, we find that nowadays a new understanding of the healing power of order is beginning to dawn not only on young people, but also for many who are in mid-career. People are rediscovering how much time they save if they apportion their days, not simply responding to the mood of the moment, but instead subjecting those moods to a self-determined order. It is especially people who are inclined to depression who sense that a daily order can be a point of security to which they can hold fast and by means of which they can straighten out their lives. For people who are weak, a fixed order can be better medicine than all sorts of psychological problem-solving, for weakness is not healed by theoretical understanding, but by bringing one's internal chaos into order. When a life acquires clear contours through external forms it will not constantly sink back into the formlessness of human immaturity. Thus it is important today that we develop new forms for our personal and communal life that are not rigid and opaque, but flexible and sensible. We can either construct such forms for ourselves or we can take advantage of those offered us by tradition. The latter have the advantage, in many cases, of having been tested over centuries and proved themselves effective.

It is not only the meditation movement that has awakened a new sensibility to forms—posture, correct sitting and standing. The many attempts to experience community anew have also discovered how effective certain rituals can be in healing common life. When the day does not begin formlessly, but with an established ritual, for example when everyone rises at the same time, begins the day with common prayer, meets others with a ritual greeting, then the day will not simply run away; it receives contours, a form out of which something can grow. What Erhart Kästner writes of the rituals of the liturgy is true also of the forms we give to our common life: "In rituals the soul feels secure. They are its solid dwelling. Here it can live . . . . The head wants what is new; the heart wants always the same thing."[4]

[4] Erhart Kästner, *Die Stundentrommel vom heiligen Berg Athos* (Wiesbaden: Insel Verlag, 1956; 5th ed. Frankfurt, 1978) 88.

BENEDICT'S UNDERSTANDING OF COMMUNITY

In modern literature we frequently encounter the human being as someone incapable of conversation. He or she talks past the other, carries on a monologue in the other's presence, feels lonely, isolated, misunderstood. He or she is not included in a community, but is "homeless," a stranger in a strange world. On the other hand, nowadays many young people sense a deep longing for community. Committed young adults have given up trying to change society through major protest demonstrations; today they want to build little worlds in which they can live in a human way. The experience of living together in a small community in which people interact intensively, discuss their problems, give each other security and "a warm nest" meets this longing. People share their funds and help each other. Many "community groups" try to work together to help others, especially the marginalized, handicapped and abandoned people, prisoners, drug addicts, migrant workers.

As idealistic as many of these goals are, the efforts often collapse. People feel overwhelmed and cannot stand the tension. They try to solve all their personal and interpersonal problems and they find that the more they try to solve them, the more problems arise. Or else the common-life group becomes a refuge that gives them security, but into which some of them retreat in order to avoid life's demands. The nest holds individuals fast and doesn't let them grow wings, doesn't let them grow up.

Everywhere today we encounter a great longing for community. Christians look to their parishes for a community that will sustain them, and they are often disappointed not to find it there. Many join clubs or political parties and hope to find there a culture of belonging. Instead, they often experience confrontation. The longing for community is continually increasing, but the experience of successful togetherness is decreasing.

In this situation a reflection on Benedict's understanding of community could reveal some essential features of successful life together. Benedict offers no theory of common life, but instead gives directions for how people can live together, in daily life and not merely in some intense emotion conjuring up a beautiful experience of community. In Chapter 72 he summarizes the demands that make common life possible:

> Just as there is a wicked zeal of bitterness which separates from God and leads to hell, so there is a good zeal which separates from evil and leads to God and everlasting life. This, then, is the good zeal which monks must foster with fervent love: *They should each try to be the first to show respect to the other* (Rom 12:10), supporting with the greatest patience one another's weaknesses of body or behavior, and earnestly competing in obedience to one another. No one is to pursue what he judges better for himself, but instead, what he judges better for someone else. To their fellow monks they show the pure love of brothers; to God, loving fear; to their abbot, unfeigned and humble love. Let them prefer nothing whatever to Christ, and may he bring us all together to everlasting life.[1]

The first demand is for respect for the other. Respectfully, I bow before the mystery of the other. I allow it to stand and refuse to try to penetrate it. I also refuse to try to change the other. Respecting the other, I believe that God loves the brother or sister and shows him or her the best path. Nowadays it is almost an addiction to want to penetrate the mystery of the other under the pretense of wanting to heal her or him. Without our noticing it, the help often consists in remaking the other according to my standards, my psychological principles,

---

[1] *RB* 72.

instead of really helping him or her. For Benedict, respect is the standard for our dealing with one another. And this respect, this reverence, is ultimately founded on faith in the presence of Christ in the brother or sister. It is therefore more than a human attitude; it is religious in nature.

The second demand flows from the attitude of respect: bearing with one another. "Bear one another's burdens" (Gal 6:2) is elevated to the status of a fundamental law of common life. The monastic is essentially a brother or sister to the other, one who bears and bears with the other. His or her first intention is not to change the other, to press him or her into a mold, but to bear with him or her. The monastic is solidary with him or her, even and especially with weaknesses. He or she bears with the other's physical weaknesses, which cannot be changed in any case, and with his or her weaknesses of character as well (lat. *infirmitates morum*).

Today many communities fail because their constant mutual demand for change is simply unsustainable. Bearing with one another is an essential element of genuine community. Of course this does not mean that one has to "swallow" everything. In his chapters on punishment Benedict showed that he also understood how to approach problems, and do so with determination, not merely in words, but with intervention. Still, he knows where the limit lies, where one can and may change something. Without the fundamental law of bearing with one another, one feels constantly under pressure to change. For there are always mannerisms and characteristics of other people that bother me.

Instead of trying to get rid of everything in the other that bothers us, we should ask ourselves whether God has not given us the unpleasant brother or sister, whether God does not mean, by means of him or her, to disturb our self-righteousness and self-assurance in order to open us up to God's love, which bears with all of us. The brothers and sisters are to obey one another and pay attention to what is useful to the others. In a community one must listen to the other, to his or her needs and desires,

feelings and moods, ideas and initiatives. Each should be atten-
tive to the other. By obedience Benedict means that I accept responsibility for the community, that I permit myself to be
challenged by the needs of the community and attend to them
instead of simply withdrawing into my own desires and needs.
My own self-realization is not to be placed above the community, for only if I open myself to a community and bind myself
to it in responsibility can I realize myself. A self-realization that
attends only to one's own needs and is indifferent to the desires
of others is an ideology. In serving, in responsibility, in obedience, in opening myself to the others, I find myself.

Benedict describes the emotional situation of the community in the Latin expression *caritatem fraternitatis caste impen-
dant*, "they should show pure brotherly love for one another."
Brotherly (and sisterly) love is to mark the community. It is a
mature love, not merely built on feelings and emotions. With
caste Benedict means a love that has gone beyond the stage at
which I project my feelings onto another and thus find myself
so emotionally bound to him or her that I am jealous of
everyone else who has contact with that person.

Benedict demands of the brothers and sisters a love that
does not exclude feelings, a love full of human warmth, but
also a love that has matured, that goes deeper than our feelings, that touches the true mystery of the other, the presence
of Christ in the brother or sister. And therefore the very basis
of brotherly/sisterly love is love for God, reverence for God's
presence in the human being. Such a love is more than feeling;
it expresses itself in concrete action. In this love the brothers
and sisters are to serve one another, says Benedict in Chapter
35 of the *Rule*, by weekly kitchen service. And he describes
service very matter-of-factly—in the kitchen, at table, clean-
ing up, caring for the sick. Just as important as an atmosphere of mutual love in a community is that the ordinary
daily services function, that people are not constantly irritat-
ing one another about the problem of washing up, that they
don't spend more time discussing the washing up than it

would take to do it. Brotherly/sisterly love, which should sustain a community, must always be concrete love, ready for the most ordinary services, and capable of organizing those activities clearly and without too much emotion.

Another element that Benedict sees as basic to his community model is love for Christ, whom one is to place above all feeling for other human beings. Christ is the foundation of a community that is capable of holding together over the long haul. Community is more than the beautiful experience of positive relationships between people. If community builds only on feelings, what results is either group egoism or disappointment and resignation, because the feelings somehow did not "work out." Jacques Loew had an experience similar to Benedict's in his basic communities:

> As we see, genuine brotherly community does not rest primarily on feelings. Like the house built on rock, it is founded on Jesus and the word of God. Does that mean that feelings have no place? Certainly not, but feelings come later, like a flower, or fruit on the tree. It is not the root of the tree. If we build a team, a community on the joy "of feeling good with each other," if our conversations are too often sprinkled with expressions like "being understood," "trusting," "I concede," "I don't want to judge," the team will always be on an insecure footing and thus will become a care that will so preoccupy us that no one will have any time or opportunity to do anything else. But if the community builds on the will to make the Lord present and to act accordingly, then the rest will happen by itself.[2]

Thus an essential precondition for the endurance of a community as it is found in the monastery is that it lives toward a goal that lies outside itself, that it places Christ above itself. That protects the community from ideologizing, something one may often observe in communities of life. Because the monastics all serve Christ together and regard him as the center of their lives, a genuine human community can arise around

---

[2] Jacques Loew, *Ihr sollt meine Jünger sein* (Freiburg: Herder, 1978) 152.

this center, one that is more enduring than feelings of trust and security.

Benedict had in mind a community of monastics. Monk, in fact, means "alone." A monk or monastic is one who lives alone, lives singly. Therefore the community, as Benedict understands it, is always marked by a fertile tension between solitariness and community. Benedict's community is not a bachelor's club dedicated to its own thriving; it is not a cozy nest like what so many seem to want today; it is a mature community, one in which individuals very deliberately face their solitariness and maintain it before God. Community is not a means to take away my solitariness; on the contrary, it is a place in which individuals consciously dare to be solitary because they see it as an essential element for human and religious maturing. The community deliberately sets apart a space for solitariness and protects it for individuals.

One fundamental feature of this solitariness is silence, which Benedict regards as an essential element of monasticism. In silence the individual separates from all ties to this world and other people in order to be open to God. For the ancient monastics, silence was a sign of our pilgrim status, a sign that we have no enduring place here where we can settle. In silence we withdraw from the world, become strangers to it, in order to learn that our true home is in heaven. Benedict creates in and through his monastic community a place of common silence, a place in which common life is repeatedly interrupted for God, before whom each individual must present herself or himself.

Benedictine monasteries are places of stillness, and that stillness is something our society needs today more than ever before. People are getting sick from constant noise. They long to dive into an atmosphere of stillness. Many single people suffer from the silence around them. For them, silence is a sign of their loneliness. The monastics create a space for silence together. They afford silence to each other so that in it they can listen to God's voice and be one with God. Silence is for them an essential element on the path of their spiritual practice. In silence they encounter themselves and in silence they let go of the cares and problems with which they often burden themselves. But the goal of silence is to become one with God, and in God to become one with all people. Thus monastics experience their aloneness as the place in which they are one with all things.

CONCLUSION

Fifteen hundred years separate us from the life of Benedict of Nursia. But a glance into his *Rule* has shown that Benedict has a message for us, extending over this enormous gap in time, a message that can show us, too, a path that has proven itself, over centuries, as a path to God and a path to the healing of humanity. We must only listen patiently, as Benedict demands of his monastics in the Prologue to the *Rule:*

> Listen carefully, my son, to the master's instructions, and attend to them with the ear of your heart. This is advice from a father who loves you; welcome it, and faithfully put it into practice. The labor of obedience will bring you back to him from whom you had drifted through the sloth of disobedience.[1]

"The master's instructions" refers not to Benedict, but to Jesus Christ, who is our true Master. We can learn from Benedict to listen to Christ anew. Benedict wanted only to expound the Gospel of Jesus Christ and translate it into a concrete way of life. He thus made an essential contribution to the Christianization of the West. He suffused the concrete aspects of life—work, prayer, community, manual labor, and art—with the spirit of the Gospel and so created a Christian way of life that still influences our Western culture. In the opening words of his *Rule* it is clear, however, that following the spiritual path that transforms this world in the spirit of Jesus is a hard task. For Benedict, spirituality is not a luxury for people who already have everything. Instead it means work, effort, honest struggle with oneself, a fight with one's

---

[1] *RB*, Prologue, 1–2.

own model of life in order to allow oneself to be shaped more and more fully by the spirit of Jesus.

For me, Benedict's message today is: "Quit complaining! The problems of the world are not there to be lamented, but to be solved. Do what you can. Build a community around you that will stand. It can be your family, your group of friends, your company, your parish. If you can create a Christian way of life where you live, it will be like leaven for this world."

Benedict did not claim to be able to change the whole world. In the midst of the confusions of his own time he set out to shape a little community in such a way that it would be filled with the spirit of Jesus. His path led over many obstacles that people put in his way. But above all, Benedict experienced the resistance of his own brothers. It is not so easy to let oneself be shaped by the spirit of Jesus. Our old patterns of life are too entrenched. But it is worth it. When a little community reflects Jesus, it will become a leaven for this world. What Jesus said and did will become visible in the concrete life of the monastics together, in their way of working and praying and in the way they deal with the things of this world.

We Benedictines cannot say that we reflect Jesus today. But we sense that it is worthwhile, in the spirit of Benedict, to follow the traces of the Gospel farther and farther and to let the spirit of Jesus become visible and tangible for people today through a grounded spirituality. And with our lives we want to make a contribution to the way in which, in many places in this world, Christians are coming together and finding joy in living together in a Christian way and building toward the future of a more human and Christian world.